MW00413854

From Exhausted to Extraordinary:

Strategies to Reverse Nurse Fatigue.

1

Renee Thompson, DNP, RN, CMSRN

FROM EXHAUSTED TO EXTRAORDINARY
Strategies to reverse nurse fatigue

Disclaimer: This book is intended for general information purposes only. For legal or psychological advice, consult on appropriate professional.

To contact the author, Renee Thompson, visit:
Website: RTConnections.com
LinkedIn: LinkedIn.com/in/rtconnections
Facebook: RTConnect/fbfollow.me
Twitter: Twitter.com/rtconnections
Blog: Blog.RTConnections.com

To contact the publisher, visit:
www.RTConnections.com

Printed in the United States of America
Paperback ISBN: 978-1519792211
e-Book ISBN: 978-1508845065
-Self Help -Personal Growth

This book is dedicated to the thousands of nurses who feel burned out at work. Nurses who sacrifice their physical, mental, and emotional health to care for others. I wrote this book to take care of them.

5

Testimonials...

"This book came along at a time when I was feeling overwhelmed, tired, and stressed! As I began to read, I immediately felt a sense of "calm" and support, knowing that I was not alone! I plan to recommend this to several colleagues and use the action steps in my daily routine. Thank you Renee for writing such an inspiring and practical guide!!"

-Nurse Keith

"This book "From Exhausted to Extraordinary: Strategies to Reverse Nurse Fatigue" is chocked full of great strategies to create an environment which is workable and supports your wellbeing. Most nurses don't realize that they may be experiencing symptoms of fatigue. We think we are super nurse and can do it all. However, nurse fatigue not only endangers the nurse but also the patient. That is why this book should be a must read for every nurse. Dr. Thompson explains exactly why fatigue sets in and simple action steps we can take to avoid the fatigue."

-Amazon Customer

"Renee's book is positive, enthusiastic, & contains real life tips for how to improve your outlook on colleagues, peers, nursing, as well as life outside the hospital. I have worked in nursing for 25+ years & can identify with each of the many examples Renee uses & support her concise, clear, & very simple tips to save yourself from the negativity of our culture. Nurses are outcome focused. I love that Renee focuses on simple, concrete steps we can take to influence our own outcomes, but at the same uses my favorite expression "Its about progress not perfection." It's a value at twice the price! Well done Dr. Thompson."

-Lorie A. Brown

"Dr. Renee Thompson knows what she's talking about. As a seasoned nurse, speaker, and educator, Renee speaks from a place of deep knowledge and experience, coupled with compassion and a true understanding of human nature and the healthcare industry. In this small but mighty book, Dr. Thompson offers savvy and realistic advice that includes motivational information, action steps, and sage words of wisdom about relationships, wellness, and the nature of 21st-century life. I cannot recommend this book highly enough for nurses who want to "up their game" when it comes to self-care, personal wellness, and improving relationships at work. Meanwhile, I also must take this opportunity to recommend Dr. Thompson as a speaker, educator, and all around stellar human being."

-Robin L. Myers

"Great start to turning around exhaustion with realistic suggestions. Especially liked the section on making your life more positive. Often times nurses awfulize without even knowing it. I truly believe that cultivating positive energy is life changing. Recommend this book. Quick read with useful suggestions that can be implemented very quickly."

~ Elizabeth Krch-Cole

"As nurses, we often have the knowledge about how to manage stress and fatigue, and we freely offer this knowledge to our patients. But so many of us don't follow our own advice when things get tough. The author reminds us of how to take care of ourselves by reviewing different techniques, breaking them down in simple steps. This ebook is a quick read, but a good reminder that nurses are important people who need to stay emotionally and psychologically healthy."

~Marijke Vroomen-Durning

TABLE OF CONTENTS

FROM EXHAUSTED TO EXTRAORDINARY:
Strategies to reverse nurse fatigue

INTRODUCTION

The unpredictability of healthcare is both exciting AND stressful. Nurses deal with life and death situations on a daily basis. Some of these situations are anticipated like the end stage COPD patient who is now in massive heart failure or the patient with a long battle with a glial brain tumor who starts to exhibit Cushing's Triad. But many times, patients crash unexpectedly. Your only "stable" patient becomes your code 15 minutes before the end of your shift. Your 94-year-old cognitively intact patient promises to pull the bathroom cord and wait for you before returning to her bed. Five minutes later you hear knocking coming from her room and a soft voice yelling, "Help. Help." You open the door to find her lying on the ground in pool of blood because she hit her head. Oh, by the way, she's on Warfarin.

We celebrate with humans when life is brought into this world and mourn with them when life is taken from them. Nurses are the common denominator from beginning to end. We are the glue that helps close the loop.

If you're like many nurses, you leave work with mixed

feelings. Sometimes we are in awe of the human spirit to persevere despite the challenges but other times we are exhausted and emotionally spent. We save lives by noticing the subtle changes in our patients' assessment and then acting on them or by fighting a physician to the "death" to get what we need for patients. And we hold a mother's hand when she is told that her 2-year has an inoperable brain tumor with 3 months to live. Nurses spend their lives caring for others yet we often suffer the consequences of that care by getting burned out.

60% of all healthcare employees report feelings of burn-out and fatigue.

If you're one of the 60%, forgive yourself. It's not your fault. However, it's time that you recognize you are burned out and DO something about it. We have a lot more work to do. Many more lives to save, hands to hold, and caring memories to make for our public.

And who is the public?

We are the public too.

What if I told you there was a way for you to get back the feeling of optimism, enthusiasm and joy of being a nurse? Would you believe me? It's true. This book is designed to teach you simple proven strategies that will help you reduce feelings of fatigue, exhaustion, and burnout.

However, what's easy to do is easy not to do. It's all up to you. I can guide you but you're the one who has to walk the path.

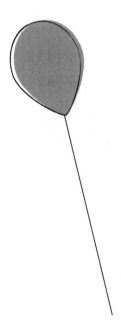

13

NURSE FATIGUE

Nurse fatigue is getting a lot of attention lately. Why? It's because studies show that when nurses get burned out, individual nurses, the nursing profession, health care organizations and ultimately patients SUFFER! When nurse don't feel good about the work they do, it impacts their ability to engage in providing high quality, effective and safe patient care. Nurse fatigue has a negative effect on work relationships and our ability to communicate assertively.

Bottom line: Nurse fatigue is badness…pure and simple badness!

What comments describe how you feel at the end of your workday?

"Yay! I had the best day ever!"
"UGH. I am so exhausted that I can't see straight!"
"Grrr. I am so angry that I want to rip someone's head off!"

If you're like many nurses, you leave work feeling exhausted, overwhelmed, or angry. You may start your day full of energy and enthusiasm but end your day feeling totally depleted. Nurses are revered as the most ethical, trustworthy profession. We sacrifice our friends, families, our backs and our bladders to take care of strangers! However, who is taking care of us? We give everything we have to our patients yet we have nothing left for ourselves.

It's time for that to change.

In this book, you will learn simple strategies to minimize exhaustion and maximize your energy so that when you leave work, you actually have energy left for your friends, your families, and yourself!

"If you are distressed by anything external, the pain is not due to the thing itself, but to your estimate of it; and this you have the power to revoke at any moment."
~Marcus Aurelius

HOW DO YOU DEFINE FATIGUE?

There are multiple terms we use to describe the same issue: nurse fatigue, compassion fatigue, burnout, and disengagement (in this book we will use the term nurse fatigue). Regardless of the term you use, they all describe the same feelings of exhaustion, feeling overwhelmed, and energy depletion.

My definition of nurse fatigue: Nurse fatigue is the combination of physical, mental, emotional, and spiritual depletion, which is caused from repeated and consistent chronic toxic stress.

My definition of stress: Stress is when you don't feel like you have the resources to meet the demands placed upon you. Whether you're a clinical nurse at the bedside, a nurse educator at a university, a nurse executive, a homecare nurse, or even a nursing student, we can all fall victims to stress when we don't believe we have the resources to meet the demands.

You get report from your co-worker and find out that two of your patients are in active alcohol withdrawal; two are active acute stroke patients and one is in isolation with a trach, copious amounts of secretions requiring suctioning and the nurse tells you he needs q1 hour IV Morphine and q2 hour IV Ativan. And, you don't have any nursing

17

assistants because they had to use them as sitters.

That was my assignment one day last year.

You're a unit manager on a busy 35-bed telemetry unit. You arrive at 6am to spend time with your night staff and stay until 6pm to finish your audits. Once you are home and finally starting to relax, your pager goes off. Apparently someone called off and the staffing office doesn't have a nurse to send you. They are asking YOU to come back to staff your unit from 11p – 7a.

Rinse and Repeat - day after day.

And now you know why nurses get burned out.

Nurse fatigue has received a lot of attention lately by The Joint Commission because studies show that when nurses feel fatigued, they make mistakes. The American Nurses Association is leading efforts to reduce nurse fatigue through a newly developed position statement, recommendations and strategies for nurses and their employers.

Why?

Because nurses have an ethical responsibility to protect

the public. When we're fatigued, we are dangerous to our public.

However, nurses don't have to be passive victims when it comes to stress. Numerous studies show that even in similar situations, some people don't succumb to the negative effects of repeated stress like others do.

Why?

Because they incorporate strategies into their daily lives that counteract the effects of stress. They equip their brains and their bodies with the tools necessary to kick the crap out of stress and burnout.

WHY ARE WE SO FATIGUED?

Many nurses have observed that the healthcare environment is getting more and more stressful and that they are being asked to do more and more with less and less, thereby, adding to feelings of not being able to keep up with the demands. This leads to chronic, toxic stress. Stress saps our energy leaving feeling exhausted.

But why is it getting worse?

It's because of interplay of three forces: People, Technology and Economics. Let me explain how each one impacts and enhances the feeling of fatigue.

People

25% of all human beings are not mentally healthy. One out of every nine humans in this country is on an anti-depressant. Have you noticed that you are caring for more and more patients with mental health issues? The mental health issues are not only present in the patients you're caring for; they are present in your co-workers too!

If you are a clinical nurse, typically the first thing you do when you come into work is to look at the assignment board. It's not necessarily to see what patients you are caring for, especially if you have been off for a few days. It is to see whom you are WORKING with. You think, "Yes! I'm working with Kim. This is going to be a great day!" Or you groan, "Oh no! I'm working with Linda!" Linda wouldn't give you the courtesy of spitting on you if you are on fire. You immediately feel stressed knowing that you can't rely on your co-workers if you need help.

Although humans are social creatures and need caring interaction, sometimes it's these other humans that cause us stress.

Technology

We are no longer in the industrial age. We are now in the information and technology age. On a daily basis, nurses are required to learn new information and new gizmos. It's hard to keep up. You feel this constant pressure to meet all of these learning and technology demands just to provide basic nursing care. Think about the introduction of the electronic health record. I remember how stressed some nurses get when asked to adopt an electronic healthcare record. Seriously. It incited mutiny! While some nurses learned (kicking and screaming) some just jumped ship! As the electronic record evolved it created more gizmos to learn to interface with. Safe medication delivery now includes a scanning device that has to be charged and cared for to make sure it works. Patient labs now print from the physician order onto a personal label machine, which also requires accuracy to print and apply labels to blood tubes. You just get comfortable using a piece of equipment or new process and it is changed again! Although these advances help to improve our ability to provide high quality, effective, safe patient care, they can contribute to a nurse's stress.

I decided to return to the bedside two years ago just to keep my "toe dipped in the water". I teach many clinical courses and didn't feel right teaching nurses about diabetes or cardiac disease when I hadn't cared for a patient in 5 years! So, I took a leap of faith and accepted a casual bedside nursing position at a hospital in my hometown of Pittsburgh. It took me six months just to master the IV pumps. Think about it. I only work 1- 2 days per month. So it took me longer to master the pump. When managing the IV pump finally became automatic for me, I read an email that we were changing pumps!!!

Technology is here to stay and that's a good thing. However, changes in technology add one more layer of stress onto nurses' shoulders.

Economics

Like it or not economics play a huge role in healthcare. Nurses are constantly being asked to do one more thing, then two more things, and now 20 more things! The Affordable Care Act, Meaningful Use, HCAHPS and patient satisfaction scores drive the work nurses do, and they are based on finances. The United States spends more than 2.6 trillion dollars on healthcare per year yet we are ranked 11th in quality compared to similar countries. Changes in reimbursements and therefore, diminishing resources for providers are aimed at decreasing costs, improving quality and ensuring all people in the United States have access to healthcare.

As nurses, we need to understand that it isn't just our managers giving us more work because they want to, it's because the financial stability of the organization depends on it.

FATIGUE SYMPTOMS

People react differently to stress, however, nurses who are fatigued report the following common symptoms: Difficulty concentrating, poor self-care, compulsive behaviors (overeating, overspending, gambling, etc.), chronic physical ailments such as GI disturbances, recurrent colds, back pain, and headache, apathy, sadness, no longer finding activities pleasurable, mentally and physically tired. It's the feeling of exhaustion at the end of your workday to the point where you feel like you have nothing left to give your family.

You work three super busy 12-hour shifts in a row. At the end of your third day, you go home so exhausted that you can't read a magazine or engage in an adult conversation. The entire next day you're on the couch recovering (twitching here and there). The next morning, you finally feel human again but you have to go back to work!

And the cycle repeats itself.

"It's not whether you get knocked down, it's whether you get up." -Vince Lombardi

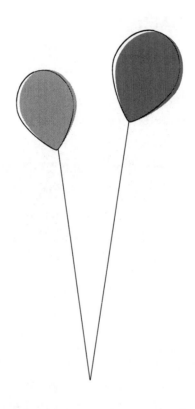

SOLUTIONS

We've discussed the definition of fatigue, why it happens, and some of the symptoms. We could continue to discuss the numerous studies regarding fatigue and its impact on patient safety, nurses and to our overall healthcare system. However, I'd rather focus on solutions!

The following represents simple strategies to reduce the impact of stress on your physical, mental, and emotional health. By incorporating just one of these strategies, you can significantly improve your energy, your career, and your personal life.

COMMIT TO PERSONAL DEVELOPMENT

As a student of human achievement/behavior and reader of almost two thousand books and articles on the topic of success, I can suggest some specific strategies to stop the fatigue syndrome and improve your energy and positivity. It's always fascinating to me how some people who start with nothing achieve so much while others who have everything waste their lives away. If you study the humans who achieve great things, they all have one characteristic in common – they commit to personal development.

The late Jim Rohn, famous business guru and consultant, said, "Formal education will make you a living. Self-education will make you a fortune." And what does that mean? When YOU commit to continuous personal and professional growth, independent of whether or not your organization requires it or pays for it, you have more control over your life, are more successful and achieve more!

I teach certification review courses and advocate for certification throughout the United States. I've listened to many nurses who think certification is a waste of time or not necessary. A nurse with 30 years experience says, "I don't need no stinking certification to prove that I'm competent!" And she's right. Certification doesn't PROVE competence. It VALIDATES it. Certification validates competence to yourself, to your co-workers, and most importantly, to your public. Patients and families know more now than ever. They ask tough and interesting questions. Are you certified is one of the frequently asked questions. Think about what happens when you go through the process of getting certified. You had to prepare. You had to study. You set your sights on a goal and focused your efforts to succeed. It makes you a better human being; it makes you a better nurse. That is the nurse I will request to care for my family.

Successful people commit to one action every day. They read.

Successful nurses (and humans) commit to reading every day – no matter what. Reading every day is the one thing I believe had the biggest positive impact on my life. Reading helped me to improve my relationships with others, grow my nursing career and eventually, start my own company. I will go without food before I go without reading. Reading is more nourishing!

Tip: *If there is a book I want to read, I get it from the library first. The library is FREE!!*

"Successful people maintain a positive focus in life no matter what is going on around them. They stay focused on their past successes rather than their past failures, on the next action steps they need to take to get them closer to the fulfillment of their goals rather than all of the other distractions that life presents to them."

-Jack Canfield

ACTION

1. Read for at least 30 minutes every day – schedule this on your calendar! Food fuels the body - reading fuels the mind. Both are required for a successful, energetic nursing career.

2. Turn your car into a mobile classroom – instead of listening to the latest hits or talk show on the radio, pop in an educational audio CD about a topic important or interesting to you.

3. Commit to attending an in-service, seminar or educational program at least once a quarter – bring a friend to increase your learning!

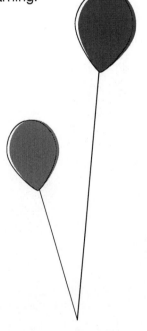

MOVE AWAY FROM NEGATIVE ENERGY

We are the average of the five people we spend the most time with; average type of house; average income; and average waist line. It's because of something in our brains called mirror neurons that mimic what they see. If I started yawning right now, everybody in the room with me would start yawning at some point, right? People from the North who move to the South experience an interesting change. Over time, they start to speak with a southern accent. It's because of mirror neurons. This is actually a survival strategy that we've adapted over time to enable us to create friendly connections with other humans.

We are born as individuals but we survive and thrive in groups. Mirror neurons are designed to connect us to each other.

Mirror neurons can work against us too. When you surround yourself with negative people and negative information, what happens to you? You become more negative.

Do you work with any energy vampires? You know, the ones who suck the life right out of you. Although we can't totally avoid negative people at work or even at home (we all have certain family members who we dread talking to!!), you can certainly set boundaries with them. Limit your time with them. If you're in the break room and they enter spewing their venom about how "horrible this place is…." leave the room. Find somewhere else to take a break or eat. The problem is, if you sit there and listen to them, you're teaching them how to treat you. That no matter what, you will listen to them rant and rave. They feel better while you feel like someone sucked the life out of you. Just say no!

Do you wake up first thing in the morning and turn on the radio or turn on the TV and listen to the murders, rapes, stabbings, and tanked economy? If so, you are polluting your brain with negativity. Remember those mirror neurons? You have to stay on guard of the doorway of your mind, and you have to surround yourself with positive people and positive things.

"You can't scratch with the turkeys if you want to fly with the eagles." -Zig Ziglar

ACTION

1. Reduce the amount of time you spend listening to negative news and watching violent television shows – beware that the media LOVES to shock the public but you've got to be smarter than the average bear.

2. Take the vampire test. After you've interacted with someone, do you feel better about yourself or worse? If you feel worse, stay away!

3. Stay out of the "Aw. Ain't it awful club" – these are the people you work with who constantly complain about everything. Don't join in!

CHOOSE YOUR ATTITUDE

People are born more positive or more negative. It's genetic. You can be born more positive but when you enter a negative environment you can become negative. Why? Remember our friends the mirror neurons? Although we just talked about how mirror neurons can work against you by mimicking the negative people and information around you, they can also help YOU become more positive.

I have a friend who is a nurse educator. She works in an office that is part of a bigger office and she walks in every day this way. There is a door and she opens up the door and she goes, "Ta da ta daaaa! I am here." Everyone claps and says, "Yay! Debbie is here!" Debbie is a positive influence on the people around her.

How do most people enter into THEIR work environment? "Blah, blah, blah…It's Monday (or, it's Saturday). I can't believe I have to be here. I was here at 11:00 at night and now I have to be here again!" How about when you walk into work and your co-workers say, "It's bad here. It's the worst day I've ever had!"

Do you think Debbie feels that great every day? She's recently gone through unbelievable tragedies in her personal life. But nobody would know it. She is always smiling and always has a positive attitude. When I asked her how she manages to stay so positive, she shared her secret. When she stands in front of the door to her office. She puts her hand on the doorknob; takes a deep breath and says to herself, "When I cross the threshold of my work environment, its game on." Because she said her nurses, her patients and everyone who enters into "her" organization deserves for her to be game on.

Attitude is a choice. Successful people make the CHOICE to have a positive attitude – no matter what.

"Happiness is not something you postpone for the future; it is something you design for the present."

-Jim Rohn

ACTION

1. When you wake up in the morning, set the intention for the day that no matter what happens, you are going to stay positive. Doing this will help to create a positive day in your subconscious mind.

2. Smile. Smiling releases oxytocin, the feel good chemicals in your brain.

3. Start a gratitude journal. Every day, write down 3 things you are grateful for. People who do this consistently over time, develop a more positive attitude! It works!

STOP MULTI-TASKING AND START PRIORITIZING!

Women think they can multi-task much better than men. Although there is actually SOME truth to that (women use both sides of their brains more efficiently - it has something to do with the corpus callosum and the way that messages cross the brain tracts), NO HUMAN can pay attention to more than one thing at a time. Yet many nurses try, leading to mental exhaustion!

You're driving in your car and you're driving somewhere you've never been before. You're listening to the radio and perhaps singing along. But as soon as you drive down the street of the house you're looking for, what do you do to the radio? You turn it down. It's intuitive. It's because you cannot pay attention more than one thing at a time.

When we multi-task, we increase our stress level and decrease our productivity.

Instead of multi-tasking, start prioritizing. Literature supports that nurses make mistakes when they try to multi-task when preparing medications, so stop doing that. Think about your big-ticket items. When you're performing certain high-risk patient procedures or giving medications, you must focus on doing one thing at a time.

And when I say prioritizing I don't mean just work. You have got to prioritize your life. How many of you suffer from that "I can't say no to anybody" syndrome? Start saying no to people who aren't key priorities in your life. The neighbor who thinks she can come over and sit and have coffee with you all day when you have one day off or the family member who you can't get off the phone with. You have got to start prioritizing your friends, your family. When you can prioritize you can start letting go of some of those negative energies.

"We can easily manage if we will only take, each day, the burden appointed to it. But the load will be too heavy for us if we carry yesterday's burden over again today, and then add the burden of the morrow before we are required to bear it."
-John Newton

ACTION

1. When you wake up in the morning, make a list of everything you need to do. Then pick the top 3 most important items. Do them first!

2. If you're a bedside nurse, for each patient, determine your "must dos" (medications, procedures) "should dos" (flush IV, update plan of care) and "could dos" (stock room with supplies, hang courtesy bags).

3. Identify high risk/high importance items ahead of time. When stressed and in the moment, it's difficult to determine what is high risk (IV medications) or high importance (grant deadlines).

STOP LETTING OTHER PEOPLE
MAKE YOU FEEL BAD

Why do we let other people who are not important in our lives make us feel bad about ourselves? You may receive 12 compliments in a day but you'll focus on that ONE critical remark someone makes. Even as a speaker, out of 1000 people 999 people think that I'm amazing but one person thinks I'm the spawn of the devil. Who do I focus on? Yep. The one person who didn't like me.

Why?

Because humans want to be liked by other humans. However, when we measure ourselves by the opinions of others, especially people who we either don't know or who aren't important in our lives, we can completely deplete our emotional energy.

When I was a new nurse I worked with Carol, an experienced nurse. Carol didn't like me and would find reasons to criticize me in front of other people. I just couldn't do anything right. One day I was trying to put an order sheet into the fax machine and I put it in the wrong way. She yanked the paper out in front of everybody and yelled, "Can't you do anything right? It's here," and then she called me stupid. I felt tears welling up in my eyes and said to myself, "Don't cry. Don't cry. Don't cry in front of all these people." A physician whom I respected saw what was happening, and he pulled me aside. He took me by the hand and said, "My dear, why would you let anybody who is not a kind, generous, intelligent human being make you feel bad about yourself?" He said, "You stand tall with your shoulders back because you are kind. You are generous. You are an intelligent human being." I never allowed Carol to affect me again.

A writer in the 1920's and 30's by the name of H.L. Mencken would receive critical letters from his readers. One day he decided to respond with a letter addressing their criticisms. He wrote, "I am sitting here in the smallest room of my house with your letter of criticism BEFORE me. Soon, it will be BEHIND me."

"Each morning when I open my eyes I say to myself: I, not events, have the power to make me happy or unhappy today."
-Groucho Marx, American comedian

ACTION

1. Self evaluate – Before allowing yourself to be open to criticism, evaluate your performance first. After I conduct a presentation or seminar, I objectively look at my performance and give myself a grade – A+, B, B-, etc. THEN, I read the evaluations.

2. When receiving criticism from anyone, ask yourself these questions, "Is this an important person in my life? Do I value this person's opinion? Does this person have good intent?"

3. Create a mental stop sign and use it whenever you feel yourself going down the rabbit hole of feeling bad. Just stop.

START CONNECTING WITH POSITIVE PEOPLE

Human beings are social beings. We all have the in-nate desire to feel connected to others. Connecting with positive people gives us energy and decreases stress. Nurses who combat fatigue see themselves as social lubricants at work, oiling the relationships we have with our co-workers, patients AND their family members. Yes we have patients and yes we deal with their families and we give medications and treatments and all these things, but we're dealing with human beings. We always want our patients to feel that we are engaged with them; that we are connected.

Remember our old friends the mirror neurons that mimic what they see? Although earlier we talked about how you will take on negative attitudes if you surround your-self with negative people, the same thing works with positive people too. If you surround yourself with people who are positive, who always seem to be happy, ener-getic, and fun, then over time, you will start to become more positive too!

Can you think of someone who you love to spend time with or work with? I bet it's someone that is positive.

I met Louise Jakubik four years ago. She is a nurse who

started her own business, NurseBuilders, a very successful pediatric education company. Louise was willing to give me advice on how to create a successful business, like hers. Louise and I hit it off right away. We had this connection with each other. Over the years she not only has become my business coach, but she has become my friend. Recently, I thought about why I enjoy spending time with Louise and then I figured it out. After I get off the phone with her or walk away from seeing her, I always feel better about myself, feel excited about the work ahead, and have the confidence to push through any challenges. Because Louise is so positive, always smiling, energetic and happy and she influences ME to feel the same way. Louise describes energy and life in this way. Every morning you wake up with your cup full. Throughout the day, work and people demands drain your cup – some more than others. The only way to fill your cup again is to get a good night's sleep, give your body nourishing foods, plenty of water AND to spend time with positive people!

Louise is a "cup filler". Find your Louise.

"Keep your thoughts positive because your thoughts become your words. Keep your words positive because your words become your behavior. Keep your behavior positive because your behavior becomes your habits. Keep your habits positive because your habits become your values. Keep your values positive because your values become your destiny"
-Mahatma Gandhi

ACTION

1. Make a list of all of the people in your circle of life. Identify which ones are more positive. Start spending more time with them and less time with the vampires.

2. Expose your brain to positive content. Read inspirational articles and books, watch feel good movies and videos.

3. Expand your circle of positive people. Deliberately seek out people who are positive. Find them. They are out there!

STOP TREATING YOURSELF POORLY

Nurses are notoriously known for caring for others yet we don't care for ourselves. When you fill your body with garbage food, sleep only 3-4 hours a night, survive on caffeine and think being busy is the same as exercise – you get garbage out.

Michael Pollan is my favorite food journalist. He wrote The Omnivores Dilemma, In Defense of Food, and Food Rules. He was asked what the best eating plan/diet was, and he said: Eat real food, mostly plants, not a lot. What does that mean?

Eat real food. How do you know if it's real food? Can you tell where it came from? I don't know how to say this, but what the heck is a Poptart? It's not real food. If your grandmother doesn't recognize it as food, don't eat it. Try to eat one ingredient foods. A potato is one ingredient. So is an apple, piece of chicken, and almonds. Avoid foods that have more than 5 ingredients and of course, processed foods and artificial sweeteners are the devil!

Mostly plants. He doesn't say don't eat meat, but he says to maintain primarily a plant based diet while incorporating meat sparingly. People who eat bacon for breakfast, lunch and dinner are setting themselves up for exhaustion and a heart attack! Start by limiting meat to one meal a day or go meatless one or two days of the week. It's easier for your GI system to digest plant-based foods. By cutting back on meat, you increase your available energy.

Not a lot. It's all about portion control. Do you really have to eat a whole bagel? Why not share half with a colleague? That Frappuccino you drink as a treat for a long, hard day – does it have to be a Venti? Why not order a tall? When you order a meal at a restaurant, ask the server to box half of it. If they won't do that ahead of time, physically divide your portions in half and ask for a box. The benefit? Lunch the next day.

I could spend all day on this topic in particular but will end with one of the most powerful books on the topic of food and energy that I've ever read. And, I happen to be friends with the author (bonus). Kathy Parry, Your Real Food Coach, wrote, *The Ultimate Recipe for an Energetic Life*. This book not only validates what I already know about the importance of nutrition but it also taught me a few things I didn't know. Seriously. Read it. Kathy's book will change your life!

Remember, what's easy to do is easy NOT to do. Start

small and don't give up until these changes have become habits.

Take time to work – it is the price of success;
Take time to think – it is the sources of power;
Take time to play – it is the secret of perpetual youth;
Take time to read – it is the foundation of wisdom;
Take time to worship – it is the highway to reverence;
Take time to be friendly – it is the road to happiness;
Take time to dream – it is hitching our wagon to a star;
Take time to love and be loved – it is the privilege of the gods.
-Unknown

ACTION

1. Sleep – if you're not getting 7 – 9 hours of sleep each night, you are depleting your body of the energy it needs to meet the demands during the day!

2. Eat real foods – try to just improve one meal at a time. For example, start with breakfast. Make a commitment to only eat real foods for breakfast – fruit, eggs (not poptarts, donuts and pastries!)

3. Exercise – just 20 minutes of intentional exercise releases endorphins and pumps oxygen rich blood to your brain and muscles.

FOCUS ON SOLUTIONS

If I told you not to think about a pink elephant, to just put the pink elephant right out of your mind. What would happen? You wouldn't be able to stop seeing a pink elephant! When you only focus on problems, you're only going to see the problems. Instead, nurses need to be solutionary, and think of solutions. Focusing on what we CAN (instead of focusing on problems) do to make our environment better even if it's on a small scale instead of focusing on problems gives us energy.

Don't wish for fewer problems. Wish for better skills to solve those problems. If you don't have those skills, put them on your list. There are books to teach you how to exercise, how to be a better communicator, how to deal with negative people, improve your finances, etc. How much do you think these books cost? Forty thousand, fifty thousand dollars? No. They're free! Go to the library and get them.

For every problem, there is a solution.
"People are always blaming their circumstances for what they are. I don't believe in circumstances. The people who get on in this world are the people who get up and look for the circumstances they want, and, if they can't find them, make them."

-George Bernard Shaw

ACTION

1. Identify 3 challenges you are facing right now (money, writing, etc). Look up the term on Amazon and identify a few books that pertain to that topic. Read the reviews, select the books you want to read and then find them at your local library. And read them!

2. Every time you are faced with a problem, immediately think "solution." Ask yourself, "What's the goal? What are the possible solutions? What's the best solution for this situation?" and then act on it.

3. Don't try to figure it out alone. Synergy exists when 2 or more people are trying to solve the same problem. The end result is better when you have input from a team!

MAKE OTHER PEOPLE FEEL GOOD

Human beings are myopic. We are very selfish and only care about ourselves. If you don't believe me, let's say someone took a picture of you with a group of people and passed it around. Who would you look at first? You would look at yourself right? Don't worry. It's not your fault. It's a survival thing because if we didn't focus on ourselves, we probably wouldn't have survived very long.

However, you can use this information to make other people feel good. I was in New York City about a year ago, had some extra time, and I needed blush. I'm not a big make up person. I have one mascara, one eyeliner, one eye shadow, and I didn't have blush for about a year. I decided it was time that I bought blush! I walked into Sephora and immediately felt overwhelmed. A woman approached and asked if I needed help. Yes! I said. This woman was very young, very heavy set, a person of color, and movie star gorgeous. I felt a bit intimated. She asked if she could help me and I said, "Well I'm looking for some blush," and she said, "Well let me see what you have." I showed her and she said, "That's actually a pretty good color for you." She opened it, grabbed a brush, put the blush on my cheeks, stepped back and said, "Beautiful." She stepped forward again, applied more blush, stepped back and said, "Beautiful." Stepped in a third time and I'm thinking, "How much blush is she putting on me?" She put it on, stepped back, and she said, "Beautiful." And all of a sudden, I started feeling beautiful! I bought that blush, and 100 dollars worth of other products from Sephora. As I was walking out with my tiny bag, all of a sudden it hit me, "Wait a second. She's a salesperson! They probably sent her to classes on how to make people feel beautiful." She's probably thinking, "I have to put blush on this old, tall skinny woman and make her feel beautiful!" And then I thought to myself - It didn't matter because I felt more beautiful that day, the next day, every day I put that blush on. And I keep going back to Sephora when I run out.

In that moment I realized that there's a lot of ugliness in the world, and a lot of crust, but there's beauty out there too. Every single person has beauty in them, and sometimes all it takes is somebody else to find it, to reach down and pull it out of that person. Sometimes we have to look real hard for some people. Even the crustiest people you work with have beauty inside them, and why not try to find a way to make other people feel good?

"Happiness is a kiss. You must share it to enjoy it."
-Bernard Meltzer

*"Let no one ever come to you without
leaving better and happier."*
-Mother Teresa #kindness

ACTION

1. Connect with one person every day – Look for reasons to compliment someone, especially at work. You never know when you'll make someone's day.

2. Tell one person that you love them – when you do, make sure you tell that person why.

3. Show gratitude to others – find one person to say thanks to, every day.

CREATE A POSITIVE ANCHOR

Lucky charms, a talisman or mantras are all thought to have magical powers. Actually, there is science behind the benefits of using an object or phrase to cope with difficult situations.

I worked with a woman who wore pearls every day as a clinical nurse. People would look at her and say, "Why do you have pearls on?" She replied, "The pearls remind me to always be a lady, and if someone decides to be mean to me, I think they're going to have a harder time being mean to a woman wearing pearls."

My grandmother (we called her Nonnie) had the most beautiful jewelry. When she died, I got some of her pins. One pin in particular is a silver flower with a pearl center. I wear this pin when I speak to large audiences. While I'm being introduced, I put my hand over Nonnie's pin, take a deep breath, and then walk onto the stage. Nonnie's pin is my talisman and gives me the confidence to do my best.

Select a phrase or two that you can use when things get tough. My last semester in a doctoral program was brutal. Every time I felt overwhelmed, I'd say to myself, "Whatever it takes." Reciting this mantra would help me refocus and just get it done – whatever it took!

A friend of mine used to say; "Resistance is futile!" anytime she was faced with something she didn't want to do. I once worked in a department of 11 employees but was cut down to three during rough economic times. However, we were still responsible for continuing the work of 11 people! We came up with a department mantra for when things got tough and would say to each other, "It's up to us to make it work. What do we have to do differently?"

Find an anchor that enables you to stay positive, focus and believe that you can succeed!

"Change your thoughts and you change your world."
-Norman Vincent Peale

ACTION

1. Identify your mantra or talisman. Whenever you're struggling, nervous, or stressed, pull out your anchor to help you cope.

2. Repeat affirmations to yourself every day that give you the strength and courage to meet the day's challenges. Say to yourself, "I can do this. I am capable. I am worthy."

3. Read something inspirational every morning and share it with your co-workers

I KNOW WHAT YOU'RE THINKING

"But you don't work in my environment. These strategies won't work in my environment - it's too toxic!" If so, the answer is clear. If your environment is that toxic, GET OUT. I know it's not easy to do but staying is not worth the physical, emotional and mental stress you will experience.

I worked in a department that was so incredibly toxic but I thought I could handle it – that I just needed to be tough and stick it out. And I did for three years until I developed temporomandibular joint disorder (TMJ) so bad that I couldn't fit a blueberry in my mouth or chew oatmeal AND was diagnosed with thyroid cancer. I was always the healthiest person I knew, however, when exposed to repeated chronic toxic stress, even if you think you can "handle it," you can't. Your body will absorb the stress and it will release it somewhere – through your body, your mind or your spirit.

If you're in a toxic environment, get out.

> *"If you want to change your life you have to raise your standards."*
> -Tony Robbins

VALUE YOURSELF AND VALUE OTHERS – you can't do it alone.

A pencil maker taught the pencil five important lessons before putting it in the box. He said,

"Everything you do will always leave a mark.

You can always correct the mistakes you make.

What is important is what's inside of you.

In life, you will undergo painful sharpenings, which will only make you better.

To be the best pencil, you must allow yourself to be held and guided by the hand that holds you."

YOU DESERVE TO FEEL GOOD ABOUT THE WORK YOU DO!

Thank you for choosing to become a nurse. Although you will have days that will challenge you beyond your imagination, you will have more days when you know you've made a difference in someone's life. Becoming a competent, confident, and successful nurse is possible when you take ownership of your practice. Taking ownership means learning the skills you need to deliver safe, effective, high quality patient care; asking for help when you don't know something; and taking full responsibility for your practice. The tips I've provided in this eBook will help you start your journey towards exemplary practice.

"Let us never consider ourselves finished nurses....we must be learning all of our lives" -Florence Nightingale

I'm cheering for your success!
Take care and stay connected.

Renee Thompson

Renee Thompson, DNP, RN, CMSRN
President and CEO of RTConnections, LLC

Top 10 Stress Relievers

When stressed, our brain stimulates our sympathetic nervous system which increases our heart rate, blood pressure AND the release of glucocorticoids (among other things). These chemicals in our bodies serve a purpose – to keep us alive when faced with danger. However, while releasing these chemicals helps you save patients' lives in a code situation, they are also released when you get your third admission of the day or find out you are working your entire shift with the queen bully!

Stress chemicals, primarily cortisol, can also damage your body if elevated for too long (chronic stress).

There are many, many proven strategies to reduce the stress response and release of cortisol. The following represents my personal favorites.

1. Power naps

Humans are actually physiologically programmed to take a nap halfway through their day. Most countries incorporate napping into their workday but in the United States, napping is frowned upon (ESPECIALLY in the workplace). However, napping for just 20 minutes recharges your battery giving you more energy, decreases your cortisol levels, and reduces stress.

2. Meditation

Humans have been practicing meditation for centuries as a way to quiet the mind. We KNOW meditation helps to reduce stress yet some people say they are way TOO stressed to sit quietly and meditate! Quieting your mind for just 10 minutes can provide hours of stress reduction.

3. Exercise

This is a no-brainer. We KNOW that exercise increases the release of endorphins – feel good chemicals in our brains like Dopamine, Serotonin, and Oxytocin. These chemicals are like stress Ninjas who slay stress hormones like Cortisol! Just 20-30 minutes of exercise daily is all you need to release the Ninjas!

4. Deep breathing exercises

Did you know that it's physiologically impossible for you to feel anxious while you are deep breathing? This is why many performers do a series of deep breathing exercises before they go on stage. Deep breathing works well before taking an exam too! Just three deep breaths is all you need.

5. Listening to music

Music tames the beast. That's because our brains are wired to respond to music. Music makes your life better.

6. Laughter

When you laugh, like exercise, you release endorphins that act as powerful stress busters!! And here's the good news – your brain doesn't know if you're laughing for real or laughing for fake. When you laugh, even if you just force yourself to laugh, you release magical stress fighting chemicals!

7. Eating healthy

We spend 50% of our energy digesting our food. But use MORE energy digesting processed, high fat, and artificially laden unhealthy foods. Eat real food – mostly plants – not a lot (Michael Pollan).

8. Asking for help

Why is it that we have to be martyrs and do everything ourselves or that by asking for help, we are admitting failure or that we are weak? Smart people ask for help to solve problems, get advice on how to handle complex situations, and they delegate appropriately to others.

9. Positive attitude

Attitude is a choice and so is your reaction to everything that happens to you – good, bad, or ugly. When you make the decision to maintain a positive attitude no matter what happens, your brain looks for a way to make that happen. Traffic jams become an opportunity to listen to an audio CD. Getting pulled to another unit gives you the chance to work with other amazing nurses.

10. Start a gratitude journal

Many successful humans swear that their lives changed when they started a gratitude journal. Every day, write down three things you are grateful for. Over time, you will FEEL more grateful, more positive, and less stressed. Start a journal today!

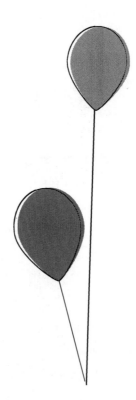

LIST OF SERVICES:

Keynote Presentations:
- **Celebrate Nursing:**
  Human by birth – Hero by choice

- **"Do No Harm" Applies to Nurses Too!**
  Strategies to eliminate bullying behavior
  in the workplace

- **From Exhausted to Extraordinary!**
  Strategies to Reverse Nurse Fatigue

Consulting:
- Anti-Bullying
- New Nurse Onboarding

Clinical Programs:
- Medical Surgical Certification Review Course
- Critical Care Certification Review Course
- Progressive Care Certification Review Course
- Emergency Nurse Certification Review Course
- Post Anesthesia & Ambulatory Perianesthesia
  Certification Review Course
- Certified Neuroscience Certification Review Course

LIST OF SERVICES: *(continued)*

<u>Leadership Programs:</u>
- **Communication, Conflict, and Coworkers - OH MY!**
  Navigating the Yellow-brick Road
  to Effective Communication

- **From Exhausted to Extraordinary:**
  Strategies to Reverse Nurse Fatigue

- **Harnessing the Power of Social Media**

- **Climbing the S.T.A.I.R.s to Preventing
  Workplace Violence:**
  Keeping Healthcare Employees Safe

- **ENOUGH: Stop the Cycle of Workplace Bullying**

<u>Products:</u>
- "Do No Harm" Applies to Nurses Too (Book)
- "Do No Harm" Applies to Nurses Too
  (DVD w/ Action Guide)
- Anti-Bullying Packages
- Conversations About Nurse Bullying (Toolkit + Book)
- Celebrate Nursing: Human by Birth,
  Hero by Choice (Book)
- From Exhausted to Extraordinary (eBook)
- Human by Birth, Hero by Choice (Thank you cards)

For more information, visit:
www.rtconnections.com/products

RESOURCES & RECOMMENDATIONS:

The following list represents resources to help you decrease stress, fatigue, and burnout:

Books
- The Ultimate Recipe for an Energetic Life, by Kathy Parry
- Brain Rules, by John Medina
- Getting Things Done, by David Allen
- Success Principles, by Jack Canfield
- The Happiness Advantage, by Shawn Achor
- Why Zebras Don't Get Ulcers, by Robert M. Sapolsky
- 7 Habits of Highly Effective People, by Stephen Covey
- Are You Fully Charged, by Tom Rath
- The No Asshole Rule, by Robert Sutton
- From Exhausted to Extraordinary: Strategies to reverse nurse fatigue, by Renee Thompson
- "Do No Harm" Applies to Nurses Too! Strategies to protect and bully-proof yourself at work, by Renee Thompson
- Celebrate Nursing: Human by Birth-Hero by Choice, by Renee Thompson

Websites
- The Energy Project: www.theenergyproject.com
- TED (Technology, Entertainment, and Design): www.ted.com
- Addicted to Success: www.addicted2success.com
- Success Magazine: www.success.com
- Kathy Parry: www.kathyparry.com
- The Chopra Center: www.chopra.com
- RTConnections: rtconnections.com
- Nursesdonoharm: nursesdonoharm.com

About the Author

Renee Thompson, DNP, RN, CMSRN
CEO and President of RTConnections, LLC

 **Dr. Renee Thompson** is a true champion for nurses. After more than 25 years as a nurse, nurse educator and nurse executive, Renee is considered a leading authority on nurse bullying, professional development, and clinical competence.

Dr. Renee Thompson is the CEO and President of RTConnections, LLC and has been repeatedly published, interviewed, and awarded for her work to educate, connect, and inspire current and future nurses. Renee is the author of several books, including *"Do No Harm" Applies to Nurses Too!, and Celebrating Nursing: Human by Birth – Hero by Choice.*

In demand as a consultant and keynote speaker, Renee helps healthcare organizations eliminate workplace bullying, develop effective communication among teams, improve clinical competence through certification, and build positive and healthy workplaces. She speaks internationally to healthcare organizations and academic institutions, teaching and motivating her audiences at conferences, training events, and seminars.

Renee received the first Outstanding Nursing Alumni for Excellence in Leadership Award from CCAC Nursing Alumni and was recently a finalist in the Healthcare Heroes Awards as a Healthcare Provider in her hometown of Pittsburgh, PA. Her blog, RTConnections, has won numerous awards as a Top Nursing Blog 'Must-Read' by the online nursing community. Her blog focuses on eliminating workplace bullying and teaching nurses how to articulate their value through ongoing professional development.

Renee has a Masters degree in Nursing Education and a Doctorate of Nursing Practice from the University of Pittsburgh. To stay connected with nurses, Renee continues to practice as a bedside nurse.

Facebook.com/rtconnections

Twitter.com/rtconnections

Blog.rtconnections.com

YouTube.com/rtconnections

LinkedIn.com/in/rtconnections

Pinterest.com/reneefava

WEBSITES:
RTConnections.com
NursesDoNoHarm.com

email: renee@rtconnections.com
phone: 412.445.2653

About RTConnections

They say that if you discover your passion, you'll never work a day in your life! That's how I feel about RTConnections. It brings me great joy knowing I'm making a difference in the lives of nurses!

At RTConnections, I offer keynote presentations, seminars and consulting services to hospitals, academic institutions and professional nursing organizations. I'm well known for my energetic and entertaining speaking style and enthusiasm for the nursing profession. Professional development and education shouldn't be boring – they should be fun!

I'm a published author of the books, "Do No Harm" Applies to Nurses Too! Strategies to protect and bully-proof yourself at work, and Celebrate Nursing: Human by Birth – Hero by Choice" and have been repeatedly published, interviewed, and awarded for my work on nurse bullying.

I spend the majority of my time traveling across the country motivating my audiences at keynote addresses and seminars. When asked what I enjoy the most, I always reply that it's meeting the most amazing nurses and nurse leaders who are out there in the muck of life trying to make a difference. It's an amazing feeling knowing that I give them the tools they need to succeed.

To stay connected with the challenges that nurses and nursing leaders face, I continue to practice as a bedside nurse. Knowing what nurses go through on a daily bases helps me to help them.

So, check out my most popular keynote presentations and seminar topics, client list, testimonials, newsletters, and award winning blog. Give me a call, shoot me an email or message me on my contact page if I can educate, connect and inspire YOUR nurses.

Take care and stay connected,

Renee Thompson

Made in the USA
Lexington, KY
21 December 2019

58846169R00046